ESOPHAGITIS DIET COOKBOOK

DELICIOUS DISHES FOR HEALING AND COMFORTING YOUR SENSITIVE ESOPHAGUS

By Archer Moore

Copyright© 2024 Archer Moore

TABLE OF CONTENTS

Living with esophagitis can be challenging, especially when it comes to mealtime. Esophagitis, characterized by inflammation or irritation of the esophagus, often requires dietary adjustments to alleviate symptoms and promote healing. This Introduction aims to provide an overview of the Esophagitis Diet Cookbook, offering guidance and support for those navigating this condition.

Understanding Esophagitis:

Esophagitis can be caused by various factors, including acid reflux, infections, allergies, or certain medications. Common symptoms may include heartburn, difficulty swallowing, chest pain, and regurgitation of food. Managing esophagitis involves not only medical treatment but also dietary modifications to reduce discomfort and promote esophageal healing.

The Importance of Diet:

Diet plays a crucial role in managing esophagitis symptoms. Certain foods and beverages can exacerbate inflammation and aggravate the condition, while others can soothe the esophagus and aid in healing. The Esophagitis Diet Cookbook is designed to provide nutritious and delicious recipes that are gentle on the esophagus, helping individuals adhere to their dietary requirements while enjoying flavorful meals.

Key Principles of the Esophagitis Diet Cookbook:

1. Soft and Easy-to-Swallow Foods: Many individuals with esophagitis find it difficult to swallow solid foods. Therefore, the cookbook focuses on recipes featuring soft textures that are easier to chew and swallow, reducing discomfort during meals.

2. Low-Acid and Non-Irritating Ingredients: Acidic and spicy foods can irritate the esophagus and worsen symptoms of esophagitis. The cookbook emphasizes ingredients that are low in acidity and non-irritating, such as lean proteins, whole grains, vegetables, and fruits with low acidity.

3. Balanced and Nutritious Meals: Maintaining a balanced diet is essential for overall health and well-being, especially for individuals managing a chronic condition like esophagitis. The cookbook offers recipes that are nutritionally balanced, providing essential nutrients while catering to dietary restrictions.

4. Variety and Flavor: Eating a monotonous diet can be dull and unappetizing. The Esophagitis Diet Cookbook aims to dispel this notion by offering a wide variety of recipes with diverse flavors and ingredients. From comforting soups and stews to satisfying main dishes and delectable desserts, there is something for every palate.

UNDERSTANDING ESOPHAGITIS: CAUSES, SYMPTOMS, AND TREATMENT

Esophagitis is a condition characterized by inflammation or irritation of the esophagus, the tube that connects the throat to the stomach. This article aims to provide a comprehensive understanding of esophagitis, including its causes, symptoms, and treatment options.

Causes of Esophagitis:

Esophagitis can be caused by various factors, including:

1. Acid Reflux (GERD): Gastroesophageal reflux disease (GERD) occurs when stomach acid flows back into the esophagus, causing irritation and inflammation over time.

2. Infections: Certain infections, such as candida (yeast) or herpes can cause esophagitis, particularly in individuals with weakened immune systems.

3. Medications: Some medications, such as nonsteroidal anti-inflammatory drugs (NSAIDs), bisphosphonates, and certain antibiotics, can irritate the esophagus and lead to esophagitis.

4. Allergies: In some cases, esophagitis may be triggered by food allergies or allergic reactions to certain substances.

5. Chemical Irritants: Exposure to chemical irritants, such as harsh cleaning agents or industrial chemicals, can also cause esophageal inflammation.

Symptoms of Esophagitis:

The symptoms of esophagitis can vary depending on the underlying cause and the severity of inflammation. Common symptoms may include:

1. Heartburn: A burning sensation in the chest, often occurring after eating or when lying down.

2. Difficulty Swallowing: Also known as dysphagia, difficulty swallowing may occur due to inflammation and narrowing of the esophagus.

3. Chest Pain: Esophageal inflammation can cause chest pain that may be mistaken for heart-related issues.

4. Regurgitation of Food: Some individuals may experience the sensation of food or liquid coming back up into the throat or mouth.

5. Nausea and Vomiting: In severe cases, esophagitis may cause nausea and vomiting, especially after eating.

Treatment of Esophagitis:

Treatment for esophagitis aims to reduce inflammation, alleviate symptoms, and address the underlying cause. Treatment options may include:

1. Medications: Proton pump inhibitors (PPIs), H2 blockers, and antacids are commonly prescribed to reduce stomach acid and alleviate symptoms of acid reflux.

2. Antifungal Medications: In cases of candida esophagitis, antifungal medications may be prescribed to treat the underlying infection.

3. Dietary Modifications: Avoiding trigger foods and beverages, such as spicy foods, citrus fruits, caffeine, and alcohol, can help reduce irritation of the esophagus.

4. Lifestyle Changes: Elevating the head of the bed, avoiding lying down immediately after eating, and maintaining a healthy weight can help reduce symptoms of acid reflux.

5. Endoscopic Procedures: In some cases, endoscopic procedures may be performed to remove obstructions, dilate narrowed areas of the esophagus, or obtain tissue samples for biopsy.

GUIDELINES FOR ESOPHAGITIS DIET

Living with esophagitis can present unique challenges when it comes to mealtime. However, with some practical guidelines and a bit of creativity, managing your esophagitis diet can become a seamless part of your everyday life. Let us humanize these guidelines to make them more relatable and accessible.

1. Listen to Your Body:

Just like tuning in to your favorite radio station, tuning in to your body's signals is essential. Pay attention to how certain foods make you feel. If something triggers discomfort or worsens your symptoms, it might be time to put it on the "skip" list.

2. Keep it Simple:

Who does not love a simple recipe that comes together in a flash? Opt for meals that are easy to prepare and gentle on your sensitive esophagus. Think smooth soups, creamy mashed potatoes, and tender steamed vegetables.

3. Embrace Variety:

Variety is the spice of life, they say! Do not let your esophagitis diet be bland and boring. Experiment with different flavors and textures to keep things interesting. One day you might enjoy a comforting bowl of oatmeal, and the next, a refreshing fruit smoothie.

4. Chew with Care:

Chewing your food thoroughly is like giving it a warm hug before it reaches your stomach. Take your time to chew each bite slowly and mindfully. This not only aids digestion but also reduces the risk of irritation to your esophagus.

5. Stay Hydrated:

Just as a plant needs water to thrive, your body needs hydration to function at its best. Sip on water throughout the day to stay hydrated and help soothe your esophagus. Herbal teas and diluted fruit juices can also be gentle alternatives.

6. Plan Ahead:

A little bit of planning, goes a long way in making mealtime a breeze. Take some time to plan your meals and snacks ahead of time. Stock up on esophagitis-friendly ingredients so you always have options on hand when hunger strikes.

7. Listen to Your Healthcare Team:

Your healthcare team is like your trusted squad, guiding you through your esophagitis journey. Do not hesitate to reach out to them for support and advice. They can provide personalized recommendations tailored to your unique needs.

8. Practice Self-Care:

Managing esophagitis is not just about what you eat, but also how you take care of yourself. Practice self-care in all aspects of your life, whether it is getting enough rest, managing stress, or enjoying activities that bring you joy.

9. Find Support:

You are not alone on this journey! Seek support from friends, family, or online communities who understand what you are going through. Sharing experiences and tips can be incredibly empowering and reassuring.

10. Celebrate Small Victories:

Every step you take towards managing your esophagitis is a victory worth celebrating. Whether it is trying a new recipe or finding a meal that brings you, comfort, acknowledge and celebrate your progress along the way.

CHAPTER 1

BREAKFAST RECIPES

CREAMY MASHED POTATOES

Serving: 4 servings   Cook Time: 25 minutes

Nutritional Information:

Serving Size: 1 cup (240g)

Calories: 210 kcal

Total Fat: 7g

Saturated Fat: 4g

Cholesterol: 20mg

Sodium: 420mg

Total Carbohydrates: 33g

Dietary Fiber: 3g

Sugars: 2g

Protein: 4g

Ingredients:

- 4 medium potatoes (about 2 pounds), peeled and cut into chunks

- 4 tablespoons unsalted butter

- 1/2 cup milk (you can use dairy-free milk for a lactose-free option)

- Salt and pepper to taste

- Optional: chopped chives or parsley for garnish

Tips for Cooking:

- Use starchy potatoes like Russet or Yukon Gold for the creamiest mashed potatoes.

- Boil the potatoes until they are fork-tender but not overly mushy, as they can become gummy if overcooked.

- Warm the milk before adding it to the potatoes to prevent them from cooling down too quickly.

- Mash the potatoes until smooth, but avoid over mixing to prevent a gluey texture.

- For extra flavor, add roasted garlic, grated cheese, or sour cream to the mashed potatoes.

Instructions:

1. In a large pot, cover the peeled and chopped potatoes with cold water. Add a pinch of salt to the water.

2. Bring the water to a boil over high heat. Reduce the heat to medium-low and simmer the potatoes until they are fork-tender, about 15-20 minutes.

3. While the potatoes are cooking, heat the milk and butter in a small saucepan over low heat until the butter is melted and the mixture is warm. Set aside.

4. Once the potatoes are cooked, drain them in a colander and return them to the pot.

5. Mash the potatoes using a potato masher or a fork until they reach your desired consistency.

6. Gradually pour the warm milk and butter mixture into the mashed potatoes, stirring until well combined and creamy. Add more milk if needed to achieve the desired consistency.

7. Season the mashed potatoes with salt and pepper to taste, adjusting as needed.

8. Transfer the creamy mashed potatoes to a serving dish and garnish with chopped chives or parsley if desired.

9. Serve the mashed potatoes hot as a delicious and comforting breakfast option.

SOFT SCRAMBLED EGGS

Serving: 2 servings   Cook Time: 5 minutes

Nutritional Information:

Serving Size: 1 serving

Calories: 160 kcal

Total Fat: 12g

Saturated Fat: 4g

Cholesterol: 370mg

Sodium: 170mg

Total Carbohydrates: 1g

Dietary Fiber: 0g

Sugars: 1g

Protein: 13g

Ingredients:

- 4 large eggs

- 2 tablespoons whole milk (you can use dairy-free milk for a lactose-free option)

- Salt and pepper to taste

- 1 tablespoon unsalted butter

- Optional toppings: chopped chives, grated cheese, diced tomatoes

Tips for Cooking:

- Use fresh, high-quality eggs for the best flavor and texture.

- Whisk the eggs and milk together until well combined but not frothy for a creamy texture.

- Cook the scrambled eggs over low to medium-low heat to ensure a soft and creamy consistency.

- Stir the eggs gently and continuously with a spatula to create small curds.

- Remove the scrambled eggs from the heat while they are still slightly runny, as they will continue to cook from residual heat.

Instructions:

1. In a medium bowl, crack the eggs and add the milk. Season with salt and pepper to taste.

2. Whisk the eggs and milk together until well combined but not frothy. Set aside.

3. Heat a non-stick skillet over low to medium-low heat. Add the butter and allow it to melt and coat the bottom of the skillet.

4. Once the butter is melted and foamy, pour the egg mixture into the skillet.

5. Using a spatula, gently stir the eggs continuously in a figure-eight motion, scraping the bottom and sides of the skillet to create small curds.

6. Continue cooking the eggs, stirring gently, until they are just set but still slightly runny, about 2-3 minutes. Be careful not to overcook the eggs, as they will become dry and rubbery.

7. Remove the skillet from the heat and let the scrambled eggs rest for a minute to finish cooking from residual heat.

8. Transfer the soft scrambled eggs to a serving plate and garnish with chopped chives, grated cheese, or diced tomatoes if desired.

9. Serve the soft scrambled eggs hot as a delicious and satisfying breakfast option.

BANANA OATMEAL SMOOTHIE

Serving: 1 serving   Cook Time: 5 minutes

Nutritional Information:

Serving Size: 1 smoothie

Calories: 280 kcal

Total Fat: 4g

Saturated Fat: 0.5g

Cholesterol: 0mg

Sodium: 100mg

Total Carbohydrates: 57g

Dietary Fiber: 7g

Sugars: 25g

Protein: 7g

Ingredients:

- 1 ripe banana, peeled and sliced

- 1/2 cup rolled oats

- 1 cup unsweetened almond milk (you can use dairy milk or any milk alternative)

- 1 tablespoon honey or maple syrup (optional for added sweetness)

- 1/2 teaspoon ground cinnamon (optional for flavor)

- Ice cubes (optional for a colder smoothie)

Tips for Cooking:

- Use a ripe banana for natural sweetness and creaminess in the smoothie.

- If you prefer a thicker smoothie, add more rolled oats. For a thinner consistency, add more milk that is almond.

- To make the smoothie colder and more refreshing, use frozen banana slices or add ice cubes before blending.

- Customize the smoothie to your taste preferences by adding ingredients like nut butter, vanilla extract, or protein powder.

- Blend the smoothie until smooth and creamy, but be careful not to over-blend as it may become too thin.

Instructions:

1. In a blender, add the sliced banana, rolled oats, almond milk, honey or maple syrup (if using), and ground cinnamon (if using).

2. If you prefer a colder smoothie, add a handful of ice cubes to the blender.

3. Secure the lid of the blender and blend the ingredients on high speed until smooth and creamy, about 1-2 minutes.

4. Pause and scrape down the sides of the blender if needed, then continue blending until all the ingredients are well combined.

5. Once the smoothie reaches your desired consistency, taste and adjust the sweetness or cinnamon if necessary.

6. Pour the banana oatmeal smoothie into a glass and serve immediately.

7. If desired, garnish the smoothie with a sprinkle of cinnamon or a banana slice on the rim of the glass.

8. Enjoy your delicious and nutritious banana oatmeal smoothie as a satisfying breakfast or snack option.

COTTAGE CHEESE PANCAKES

Serving: 2 servings (4 pancakes total)   Cook Time: 15 minutes

Nutritional Information:

Serving Size: 2 pancakes

Calories: 210 kcal

Total Fat: 9g

Saturated Fat: 4g

Cholesterol: 170mg

Sodium: 480mg

Total Carbohydrates: 13g

Dietary Fiber: 1g

Sugars: 4g

Protein: 20g

Ingredients:

- 1 cup cottage cheese

- 2 large eggs

- 1/4 cup all-purpose flour (you can use almond flour or oat flour for a gluten-free option)

- 1 tablespoon honey or maple syrup (optional for added sweetness)

- 1/2 teaspoon vanilla extract

- 1/4 teaspoon ground cinnamon (optional for flavor)

- Butter or cooking spray for greasing the pan

Tips for Cooking:

- Use full-fat cottage cheese for a creamier texture and richer flavor in the pancakes.

- Blend the cottage cheese in a blender or food processor until smooth before adding it to the pancake batter for a smoother consistency.

- Let the pancake batter rest for a few minutes after mixing to allow the flour to hydrate and the flavors to meld.

- Cook the pancakes over medium-low heat to prevent them from burning and ensure even cooking.

- Flip the pancakes when bubbles form on the surface and the edges look set, about 2-3 minutes per side.

- Serve the pancakes warm with your favorite toppings, such as fresh fruit, Greek yogurt, or a drizzle of honey or maple syrup.

Instructions:

1. In a mixing bowl, combine the cottage cheese, eggs, flour, honey or maple syrup (if using), vanilla extract, and ground cinnamon (if using). Stir until well combined.

2. Let the pancake batter rest for 5 minutes to allow the flavors to meld and the flour to hydrate.

3. Heat a non-stick skillet or griddle over medium-low heat. Lightly grease the skillet with butter or cooking spray.

4. Once the skillet is hot, pour about 1/4 cup of the pancake batter onto the skillet to form each pancake. Use the back of a spoon to spread the batter into a circular shape if needed.

5. Cook the pancakes for 2-3 minutes on the first side, or until bubbles form on the surface and the edges look set.

6. Carefully flip the pancakes with a spatula and cook for an additional 2-3 minutes on the second side, or until golden brown and cooked through.

7. Transfer the cooked pancakes to a plate and keep warm while you cook the remaining pancakes with the remaining batter.

8. Serve the cottage cheese pancakes warm with your favorite toppings and enjoy a delicious and protein-packed breakfast!

BLUEBERRY BANANA SMOOTHIE BOWL

Serving: 1 serving   Preparation Time: 5 minutes

Nutritional Information:

Serving Size: 1 smoothie bowl

Calories: 280 kcal

Total Fat: 4g

Saturated Fat: 0.5g

Cholesterol: 0mg

Sodium: 70mg

Total Carbohydrates: 57g

Dietary Fiber: 8g

Sugars: 30g

Protein: 6g

Ingredients:

- 1 ripe banana, peeled and frozen

- 1/2 cup frozen blueberries

- 1/4 cup plain Greek yogurt (you can use dairy-free yogurt for a vegan option)

- 1/4 cup almond milk (you can use any milk or milk alternative)

- 1 tablespoon honey or maple syrup (optional for added sweetness)

- Toppings: sliced banana, fresh blueberries, granola, chia seeds, shredded coconut, sliced almonds

Tips for Cooking:

- Use ripe bananas for natural sweetness and a creamy texture in the smoothie bowl.

- Freeze the banana slices and blueberries ahead of time to create a thicker and colder smoothie bowl.

- Adjust the amount of almond milk to achieve your desired consistency. Start with less milk for a thicker smoothie bowl and add more if needed.

- Customize the smoothie bowl with your favorite toppings, such as fresh fruit, nuts, seeds, or granola, for added flavor and texture.

- Blend the smoothie until smooth and creamy, scraping down the sides of the blender as needed to ensure all ingredients are well incorporated.

Instructions:

1. In a blender, combine the frozen banana slices, frozen blueberries, Greek yogurt, almond milk, and honey or maple syrup (if using).

2. Blend the ingredients on high speed until smooth and creamy, stopping to scrape down the sides of the blender as needed.

3. Pause and check the consistency of the smoothie. If it is too thick, add a splash of almond milk and blend again until desired consistency is reached.

4. Once the smoothie is smooth and creamy, pour it into a bowl.

5. Arrange your desired toppings, such as sliced banana, fresh blueberries, granola, chia seeds, shredded coconut, and sliced almonds, on top of the smoothie bowl.

6. Serve the blueberry banana smoothie bowl immediately and enjoy a delicious and nutritious breakfast that is packed with antioxidants, fiber, and protein!

SOFT QUINOA PORRIDGE

Serving: 1 serving   Cook Time: 20 minutes

Nutritional Information:

Serving Size: 1 serving

Calories: 220 kcal

Total Fat: 6g

Saturated Fat: 1g

Cholesterol: 0mg

Sodium: 160mg

Total Carbohydrates: 36g

Dietary Fiber: 5g

Sugars: 4g

Protein: 8g

Ingredients:

- 1/4 cup quinoa, rinsed and drained

- 1 cup water

- 1/2 cup unsweetened almond milk (you can use any milk or milk alternative)

- 1/2 teaspoon ground cinnamon

- 1 tablespoon honey or maple syrup (optional for added sweetness)

- Toppings: sliced banana, chopped nuts, dried fruit, shredded coconut, honey or maple syrup

Tips for Cooking:

- Rinse the quinoa thoroughly under cold water before cooking to remove any bitterness.

- Use a 1:2 ratio of quinoa to water for a soft and creamy porridge consistency.

- Cook the quinoa in water until it is tender and the water has been absorbed, about 15-20 minutes.

- Add almond milk and ground cinnamon to the cooked quinoa for added creaminess and flavor.

- Sweeten the porridge with honey or maple syrup to taste, or leave it unsweetened if preferred.

- Customize the porridge with your favorite toppings, such as sliced banana, chopped nuts, dried fruit, shredded coconut, or a drizzle of honey or maple syrup, for added texture and flavor.

Instructions:

1. In a small saucepan, combine the rinsed and drained quinoa with water. Bring the mixture to a boil over medium-high heat.

2. Once the water is boiling, reduce the heat to low and cover the saucepan with a lid. Simmer the quinoa for 15-20 minutes, or until the water is absorbed and the quinoa is tender.

3. Once the quinoa is cooked, remove the saucepan from the heat and let it sit, covered, for 5 minutes.

4. After resting, fluff the quinoa with a fork and stir in the almond milk and ground cinnamon until well combined.

5. If desired, sweeten the quinoa porridge with honey or maple syrup to taste, stirring until evenly distributed.

6. Transfer the soft quinoa porridge to a serving bowl and top with your favorite toppings, such as sliced banana, chopped nuts, dried fruit, shredded coconut, or a drizzle of honey or maple syrup.

7. Serve the quinoa porridge warm and enjoy a wholesome and nutritious breakfast that is packed with protein, fiber, and essential nutrients!

CHAPTER 2

LUNCH RECIPES

RICE CONGEE WITH CHICKEN

Serving: 4 servings   Cook Time: 1 hour 30 minutes

Nutritional Information:

Serving Size: 1 serving

Calories: 280 kcal

Total Fat: 6g

Saturated Fat: 1.5g

Cholesterol: 45mg

Sodium: 780mg

Total Carbohydrates: 40g

Dietary Fiber: 2g

Sugars: 1g

Protein: 18g

Ingredients:

- 1 cup white rice, rinsed

- 6 cups water or chicken broth

- 1 boneless, skinless chicken breast, thinly sliced

- 2 slices ginger

- Salt to taste

- Optional toppings: chopped green onions, cilantro, sliced mushrooms, shredded chicken, fried shallots, soy sauce, sesame oil

Tips for Cooking:

- Use a ratio of 1 cup rice to 6 cups water or chicken broth for a thick and creamy congee consistency.

- Rinse the rice thoroughly under cold water before cooking to remove excess starch and prevent the congee from becoming too thick.

- Add thinly sliced ginger to the cooking liquid for added flavor and aroma.

- Cook the congee over low heat, stirring occasionally, to prevent it from sticking to the bottom of the pot and burning.

- Adjust the seasoning with salt to taste before serving.

- Customize the congee with your favorite toppings for added texture and flavor.

Instructions:

1. In a large pot, combine the rinsed white rice and water or chicken broth. Add the thinly sliced chicken breast and ginger slices to the pot.

2. Bring the mixture to a boil over high heat, and then reduce the heat to low to maintain a gentle simmer.

3. Cook the congee, uncovered, stirring occasionally, for 1 hour, or until the rice grains have broken down and the mixture has thickened to a creamy consistency.

4. If the congee becomes too thick during cooking, add more water or chicken broth as needed to reach the desired consistency.

5. Once the congee is cooked to your liking, remove the ginger slices and discard.

6. Season the congee with salt to taste, stirring until evenly distributed.

7. Ladle the hot congee into serving bowls and top with your favorite toppings, such as chopped green onions, cilantro, sliced mushrooms, shredded chicken, fried shallots, soy sauce, or sesame oil.

8. Serve the rice congee with chicken hot and enjoy a comforting and nourishing lunch that is rich in flavor and texture!

TURKEY MEATBALLS IN TOMATO SAUCE

Serving: 4 servings   Cook Time: 30 minutes

Nutritional Information:

Serving Size: 3 meatballs with sauce

Calories: 250 kcal

Total Fat: 12g

Saturated Fat: 3g

Cholesterol: 80mg

Sodium: 560mg

Total Carbohydrates: 12g

Dietary Fiber: 2g

Sugars: 5g

Protein: 23g

Ingredients:

- 1 pound ground turkey

- 1/2 cup breadcrumbs (you can use gluten-free breadcrumbs if needed)

- 1/4 cup grated Parmesan cheese

- 1 large egg

- 2 cloves garlic, minced

- 1 teaspoon dried oregano

- 1/2 teaspoon dried basil

- Salt and pepper to taste

- 2 tablespoons olive oil

- 1 can (14 ounces) crushed tomatoes

- 1 teaspoon sugar

- 1/2 teaspoon dried thyme

- Optional: chopped fresh parsley for garnish

Tips for Cooking:

- Use lean ground turkey for healthier meatballs with less fat content.

- Combine the ground turkey with breadcrumbs, Parmesan cheese, egg, minced garlic, dried oregano, dried basil, salt, and pepper in a mixing bowl until well combined.

- Shape the turkey mixture into evenly sized meatballs for even cooking.

- Brown the meatballs in olive oil in a skillet over medium heat before adding them to the tomato sauce for added flavor and texture.

- Simmer the meatballs in the tomato sauce over low heat until they are cooked through and the sauce has thickened.

- Season the tomato sauce with sugar, dried thyme, salt, and pepper to taste, adjusting as needed.

Instructions:

1. In a large mixing bowl, combine the ground turkey, breadcrumbs, grated Parmesan cheese, egg, minced garlic, dried oregano, dried basil, salt, and pepper. Mix until all the ingredients are evenly incorporated.

2. Shape the turkey mixture into meatballs, using about 1 tablespoon of mixture for each meatball. Roll the mixture between your hands to form evenly sized meatballs.

3. Heat olive oil in a large skillet over medium heat. Add the meatballs to the skillet and cook until browned on all sides, about 6-8 minutes.

4. While the meatballs are cooking, prepare the tomato sauce. In a separate saucepan, combine the crushed tomatoes, sugar, dried thyme, salt, and pepper. Bring the mixture to a simmer over medium heat.

5. Once the meatballs are browned, transfer them to the saucepan with the tomato sauce. Reduce the heat to low and simmer the meatballs in the sauce for 15-20 minutes, or until they are cooked through and the sauce has thickened slightly.

6. Taste the tomato sauce and adjust the seasoning with salt, pepper, and additional herbs if needed.

7. Serve the turkey meatballs in tomato sauce hot, garnished with chopped fresh parsley if desired.

8. Enjoy these flavorful and satisfying turkey meatballs as a delicious lunchtime meal served over pasta or with crusty bread for dipping!

VEGETABLE SOUP WITH RICE

Serving: 4 servings   Cook Time: 30 minutes

Nutritional Information:

Serving Size: 3 meatballs with sauce

Calories: 310 kcal

Total Fat: 18g

Saturated Fat: 6g

Cholesterol: 95mg

Sodium: 680mg

Total Carbohydrates: 14g

Dietary Fiber: 3g

Sugars: 7g

Protein: 23g

Ingredients:

- 1 pound ground turkey

- 1/2 cup breadcrumbs (you can use gluten-free breadcrumbs if needed)

- 1/4 cup grated Parmesan cheese

- 1 large egg

- 2 cloves garlic, minced

- 1 teaspoon dried oregano

- 1/2 teaspoon dried basil

- Salt and pepper to taste

- 2 tablespoons olive oil

- 1 can (14 ounces) crushed tomatoes

- 1 teaspoon sugar

- 1/2 teaspoon dried thyme

- Optional: chopped fresh parsley for garnish

Tips for Cooking:

- Use lean ground turkey for healthier meatballs with less fat content.

- Combine the ground turkey with breadcrumbs, Parmesan cheese, egg, minced garlic, dried oregano, dried basil, salt, and pepper in a mixing bowl until well combined.

- Shape the turkey mixture into evenly sized meatballs for even cooking.

- Brown the meatballs in olive oil in a skillet over medium heat before adding them to the tomato sauce for added flavor and texture.

- Simmer the meatballs in the tomato sauce over low heat until they are cooked through and the sauce has thickened.

- Season the tomato sauce with sugar, dried thyme, salt, and pepper to taste, adjusting as needed.

Instructions:

1. In a large mixing bowl, combine the ground turkey, breadcrumbs, grated Parmesan cheese, egg, minced garlic, dried oregano, dried basil, salt, and pepper. Mix until all the ingredients are evenly incorporated.

2. Shape the turkey mixture into meatballs, using about 1 tablespoon of mixture for each meatball. Roll the mixture between your hands to form evenly sized meatballs.

3. Heat olive oil in a large skillet over medium heat. Add the meatballs to the skillet and cook until browned on all sides, about 6-8 minutes.

4. While the meatballs are cooking, prepare the tomato sauce. In a separate saucepan, combine the crushed tomatoes, sugar, dried thyme, salt, and pepper. Bring the mixture to a simmer over medium heat.

5. Once the meatballs are browned, transfer them to the saucepan with the tomato sauce. Reduce the heat to low and simmer the meatballs in the sauce for 15-20 minutes, or until they are cooked through and the sauce has thickened slightly.

6. Taste the tomato sauce and adjust the seasoning with salt, pepper, and additional herbs if needed.

7. Serve the turkey meatballs in tomato sauce hot, garnished with chopped fresh parsley if desired.

8. Enjoy these flavorful and satisfying turkey meatballs as a delicious lunchtime meal served over pasta or with crusty bread for dipping!

AVOCADO AND CHICKEN SALAD

Serving: 2 servings   Preparation Time: 15 minutes   Cook Time: 15 minutes

Nutritional Information:

Serving Size: 1 serving

Calories: 350 kcal

Total Fat: 22g

Saturated Fat: 3g

Cholesterol: 70mg

Sodium: 450mg

Total Carbohydrates: 12g

Dietary Fiber: 7g

Sugars: 2g

Protein: 28g

Ingredients:

- 2 boneless, skinless chicken breasts

- 1 avocado, diced

- 1/4 cup cherry tomatoes, halved

- 1/4 cup cucumber, diced

- 2 cups mixed greens (such as spinach, arugula, or lettuce)

- 1/4 cup red onion, thinly sliced

- 2 tablespoons olive oil

- 1 tablespoon lemon juice

- Salt and pepper to taste

- Optional: crumbled feta cheese, chopped fresh herbs (such as parsley or cilantro)

Tips for Cooking:

- Season the chicken breasts with salt, pepper, and any desired herbs or spices before cooking for added flavor.

- Cook the chicken breasts over medium-high heat in a skillet or grill until they are cooked through and no longer pink in the center, about 6-8 minutes per side.

- Let the cooked chicken breasts rest for a few minutes before slicing them thinly for the salad.

- Use ripe avocado for creaminess and flavor in the salad.

- Toss the salad ingredients with olive oil, lemon juice, salt, and pepper just before serving to keep the greens fresh and vibrant.

- Customize the salad with your favorite toppings and dressings for added flavor and texture.

Instructions:

1. Season the chicken breasts with salt, pepper, and any desired herbs or spices.

2. Heat olive oil in a skillet over medium-high heat. Add the seasoned chicken breasts to the skillet and cook until they are golden brown and cooked through, about 6-8 minutes per side.

3. Once the chicken breasts are cooked through, remove them from the skillet and let them rest for a few minutes before slicing them thinly.

4. In a large mixing bowl, combine the diced avocado, cherry tomatoes, cucumber, mixed greens, and thinly sliced red onion.

5. Add the sliced chicken breasts to the bowl with the salad ingredients.

6. Drizzle the salad with olive oil and lemon juice, then season with salt and pepper to taste. Toss gently to coat all the ingredients evenly.

7. Divide the avocado and chicken salad between serving plates or bowls.

8. If desired, garnish the salad with crumbled feta cheese and chopped fresh herbs, such as parsley or cilantro.

9. Serve the avocado and chicken salad immediately and enjoy a fresh and flavorful lunch that is packed with protein and healthy fats!

LENTIL SOUP WITH SPINACH

Serving: 6 servings   Preparation Time: 10 minutes

Cook Time: 40 minutes   Serving Size: 1 cup

Nutritional Information:

Calories: 180 kcal

Total Fat: 1g

Saturated Fat: 0g

Cholesterol: 0mg

Sodium: 480mg

Total Carbohydrates: 33g

Dietary Fiber: 8g

Sugars: 3g

Protein: 10g

Ingredients:

- 1 cup dried green lentils, rinsed and drained

- 6 cups vegetable broth or water

- 1 onion, diced

- 2 carrots, diced

- 2 celery stalks, diced

- 2 cloves garlic, minced

- 1 teaspoon ground cumin

- 1 teaspoon ground coriander

- 1/2 teaspoon paprika

- 1 bay leaf

- Salt and pepper to taste

- 4 cups fresh spinach leaves

- 2 tablespoons lemon juice

- Optional: chopped fresh parsley for garnish

Tips for Cooking:

- Rinse the dried lentils thoroughly under cold water before cooking to remove any debris.

- Use vegetable broth instead of water for added flavor in the soup.

- Sauté the diced onion, carrots, celery, and garlic in olive oil before adding the lentils and broth for enhanced flavor.

- Add ground cumin, ground coriander, paprika, and a bay leaf to the soup for aromatic and flavorful seasoning.

- Simmer the soup over low heat until the lentils are tender, about 30-35 minutes, stirring occasionally.

- Stir in fresh spinach leaves and lemon juice just before serving to retain their vibrant color and freshness.

Instructions:

1. In a large pot, combine the rinsed and drained dried green lentils with vegetable broth or water.

2. Add diced onion, carrots, celery, minced garlic, ground cumin, ground coriander, paprika, and a bay leaf to the pot.

3. Bring the mixture to a boil over high heat, then reduce the heat to low and simmer for 30-35 minutes, or until the lentils are tender, stirring occasionally.

4. Once the lentils are tender, season the soup with salt and pepper to taste.

5. Stir in fresh spinach leaves and lemon juice, allowing the spinach to wilt slightly in the hot soup.

6. Taste the soup and adjust the seasoning with additional salt, pepper, or lemon juice if needed.

7. Ladle the lentil soup with spinach into serving bowls and garnish with chopped fresh parsley if desired.

8. Serve the soup hot and enjoy a comforting and nutritious lunch that is packed with protein, fiber, and essential nutrients!

TURKEY CHILI WITH SWEET POTATOES

Serving: 6 servings   Preparation Time: 15 minutes   Cook Time: 45 minutes

Nutritional Information:

Serving Size: 1 cup

Calories: 280 kcal

Total Fat: 8g

Saturated Fat: 2g

Cholesterol: 45mg

Sodium: 600mg

Total Carbohydrates: 35g

Dietary Fiber: 7g

Sugars: 9g

Protein: 20g

Ingredients:

- 1 tablespoon olive oil

- 1 onion, diced

- 2 cloves garlic, minced

- 1 pound ground turkey

- 2 sweet potatoes, peeled and diced

- 1 can (14 ounces) diced tomatoes

- 1 can (14 ounces) black beans, drained and rinsed

- 1 can (14 ounces) kidney beans, drained and rinsed

- 2 cups vegetable broth

- 2 teaspoons chili powder

- 1 teaspoon ground cumin

- 1/2 teaspoon smoked paprika

- Salt and pepper to taste

- Optional toppings: shredded cheese, chopped cilantro, avocado slices, Greek yogurt

Tips for Cooking:

- Use lean ground turkey for a healthier chili with less fat content.

- Sauté the diced onion and minced garlic in olive oil until softened and fragrant before adding the ground turkey and sweet potatoes.

- Cook the ground turkey until it is no longer pink, breaking it up with a spoon as it cooks.

- Add diced tomatoes, black beans, kidney beans, vegetable broth, and spices to the chili for flavor and texture.

- Simmer the chili over low heat until the sweet potatoes are tender and the flavors have melded together, stirring occasionally.

- Customize the chili with your favorite toppings, such as shredded cheese, chopped cilantro, avocado slices, or Greek yogurt, for added flavor and texture.

Instructions:

1. Heat olive oil in a large pot over medium heat. Add diced onion and minced garlic to the pot and cook until softened and fragrant, about 5 minutes.

2. Add ground turkey to the pot and cook, breaking it up with a spoon, until it is no longer pink, about 5-7 minutes.

3. Stir in diced sweet potatoes, diced tomatoes (including their juices), black beans, kidney beans, vegetable broth, chili powder, ground cumin, smoked paprika, salt, and pepper.

4. Bring the mixture to a boil, then reduce the heat to low and simmer, covered, for 30-35 minutes, or until the sweet potatoes are tender, stirring occasionally.

5. Taste the chili and adjust the seasoning with additional salt, pepper, chili powder, or cumin if needed.

6. Ladle the turkey chili with sweet potatoes into serving bowls and top with your favorite toppings, such as shredded cheese, chopped cilantro, avocado slices, or Greek yogurt.

7. Serve the chili hot and enjoy a hearty and flavorful lunch that is packed with protein, fiber, and essential nutrients!

CHAPTER 3

DINNER RECIPES

BAKED CHICKEN BREAST WITH HERBS

Serving: 4 servings   Preparation Time: 10 minutes   Cook Time: 25 minutes

Nutritional Information:

Serving Size: 1 chicken breast

Calories: 220 kcal

Total Fat: 6g

Saturated Fat: 1.5g

Cholesterol: 85mg

Sodium: 400mg

Total Carbohydrates: 0g

Dietary Fiber: 0g

Sugars: 0g

Protein: 40g

Ingredients:

- 4 boneless, skinless chicken breasts

- 2 tablespoons olive oil

- 2 cloves garlic, minced

- 1 teaspoon dried thyme

- 1 teaspoon dried rosemary

- 1 teaspoon dried sage

- Salt and pepper to taste

- Optional: lemon wedges for serving

Tips for Cooking:

- Preheat the oven before baking the chicken breasts to ensure even cooking.

- Rub the chicken breasts with olive oil and minced garlic for added flavor and moisture.

- Season the chicken breasts generously with dried thyme, dried rosemary, dried sage, salt, and pepper for aromatic and flavorful herbs.

- Bake the chicken breasts in a preheated oven at 400°F (200°C) until they reach an internal temperature of 165°F (75°C) for safe consumption.

- Let the baked chicken breasts rest for a few minutes before slicing and serving to allow the juices to redistribute and the meat to stay tender and moist.

- Serve the baked chicken breasts with lemon wedges for a fresh and citrusy flavor.

Instructions:

1. Preheat the oven to 400°F (200°C). Line a baking sheet with parchment paper or aluminum foil for easy cleanup.

2. Place the boneless, skinless chicken breasts on the prepared baking sheet, making sure they are evenly spaced apart.

3. Drizzle olive oil over the chicken breasts, and then rub them with minced garlic, ensuring they are coated evenly on both sides.

4. In a small bowl, mix together dried thyme, dried rosemary, dried sage, salt, and pepper. Sprinkle the herb mixture generously over the chicken breasts, covering them completely.

5. Bake the chicken breasts in the preheated oven for 20-25 minutes or until they reach an internal temperature of 165°F (75°C) when tested with a meat thermometer.

6. Once the chicken breasts are cooked through, remove them from the oven and let them rest on the baking sheet for 5 minutes.

7. Slice the baked chicken breasts diagonally and serve hot, garnished with lemon wedges if desired.

8. Enjoy these flavorful and tender baked chicken breasts with herbs as a delicious and satisfying dinner option!

QUINOA PILAF WITH ROASTED VEGETABLES

Serving: 4 servings   Preparation Time: 15 minutes   Cook Time: 25 minutes

Nutritional Information:

Serving Size: 1 cup

Calories: 250 kcal

Total Fat: 8g

Saturated Fat: 1g

Cholesterol: 0mg

Sodium: 350mg

Total Carbohydrates: 40g

Dietary Fiber: 7g

Sugars: 5g

Protein: 8g

Ingredients:

- 1 cup quinoa, rinsed

- 2 cups vegetable broth or water

- 1 tablespoon olive oil

- 1 onion, diced

- 2 cloves garlic, minced

- 2 carrots, diced

- 1 bell pepper, diced

- 1 zucchini, diced

- 1 cup cherry tomatoes, halved

- 1 teaspoon dried thyme

- 1 teaspoon dried rosemary

- Salt and pepper to taste

- Optional: chopped fresh parsley for garnish

Tips for Cooking:

- Rinse the quinoa thoroughly under cold water before cooking to remove any bitterness.

- Use vegetable broth instead of water to cook the quinoa for added flavor.

- Sauté the diced onion and minced garlic in olive oil until softened and fragrant before adding the quinoa and broth.

- Roast the diced vegetables in the oven until they are tender and caramelized for added flavor and texture in the pilaf.

- Season the quinoa pilaf with dried thyme, dried rosemary, salt, and pepper for aromatic and flavorful herbs.

- Garnish the quinoa pilaf with chopped fresh parsley for a pop of color and freshness before serving.

Instructions:

1. Preheat the oven to 400°F (200°C). Line a baking sheet with parchment paper or aluminum foil for easy cleanup.

2. In a medium saucepan, combine the rinsed quinoa and vegetable broth or water. Bring the mixture to a boil over high heat.

3. Once boiling, reduce the heat to low, cover the saucepan with a lid, and simmer the quinoa for 15-20 minutes, or until all the liquid is absorbed and the quinoa is tender. Remove the saucepan from the heat and let it sit, covered, for 5 minutes. Fluff the quinoa with a fork.

4. While the quinoa is cooking, prepare the roasted vegetables. Place the diced carrots, bell pepper, zucchini, and cherry tomatoes on the prepared baking sheet. Drizzle with olive oil and sprinkle with dried thyme, dried rosemary, salt, and pepper. Toss to coat the vegetables evenly.

5. Roast the vegetables in the preheated oven for 15-20 minutes, or until they are tender and caramelized, stirring halfway through cooking.

6. In a large skillet, heat olive oil over medium heat. Add diced onion and minced garlic to the skillet and cook until softened and fragrant, about 5 minutes.

7. Add the cooked quinoa and roasted vegetables to the skillet with the onion and garlic. Stir to combine and heat through.

8. Taste the quinoa pilaf and adjust the seasoning with additional salt and pepper if needed.

9. Garnish the quinoa pilaf with chopped fresh parsley before serving.

10. Serve the quinoa pilaf with roasted vegetables hot as a flavorful and nutritious dinner option!

BAKED SWEET POTATO FRIES

Serving: 4 servings   Preparation Time: 10 minutes   Cook Time: 25 minutes

Nutritional Information:

Serving Size: 1 cup (about 150g)

Calories: 160 kcal

Total Fat: 5g

Saturated Fat: 0.5g

Cholesterol: 0mg

Sodium: 180mg

Total Carbohydrates: 28g

Dietary Fiber: 4g

Sugars: 5g

Protein: 2g

Ingredients:

- 2 large sweet potatoes, washed and scrubbed

- 2 tablespoons olive oil

- 1 teaspoon paprika

- 1/2 teaspoon garlic powder

- 1/2 teaspoon onion powder

- 1/2 teaspoon salt

- 1/4 teaspoon black pepper

- Optional: chopped fresh parsley for garnish

Tips for Cooking:

- Choose large sweet potatoes with smooth, unblemished skins for the best results.

- Cut the sweet potatoes into uniform-sized fries to ensure even cooking.

- Soak the cut sweet potato fries in cold water for 30 minutes to remove excess starch and help them crisp up when baked.

- Pat the soaked sweet potato fries dry with paper towels before tossing them with olive oil and seasonings to ensure they bake evenly and become crispy.

- Arrange the sweet potato fries in a single layer on a baking sheet lined with parchment paper or aluminum foil to prevent them from sticking and to promote even browning.

- Bake the sweet potato fries at a high temperature (around 425°F/220°C) for crispy results, flipping them halfway through cooking to ensure they cook evenly on all sides.

Instructions:

1. Preheat the oven to 425°F (220°C). Line a baking sheet with parchment paper or aluminum foil for easy cleanup.

2. Cut the washed and scrubbed sweet potatoes into uniform-sized fries, about 1/4 inch thick.

3. Place the cut sweet potato fries in a large bowl and cover them with cold water. Let them soak for 30 minutes to remove excess starch.

4. After soaking, drain the sweet potato fries and pat them dry with paper towels.

5. In the same bowl, toss the dried sweet potato fries with olive oil, paprika, garlic powder, onion powder, salt, and black pepper until evenly coated.

6. Arrange the seasoned sweet potato fries in a single layer on the prepared baking sheet, making sure they are not overcrowded.

7. Bake the sweet potato fries in the preheated oven for 20-25 minutes, flipping them halfway through cooking, until they are golden brown and crispy.

8. Once baked, remove the sweet potato fries from the oven and let them cool slightly on the baking sheet.

9. Garnish the baked sweet potato fries with chopped fresh parsley if desired, and then serve them hot as a delicious and nutritious dinner side dish or snack.

GINGER CARROT SOUP

Serving: 4 servings   Preparation Time: 10 minutes   Cook Time: 25 minutes

Nutritional Information:

Serving Size: 1 cup

Calories: 120 kcal

Total Fat: 3g

Saturated Fat: 0g

Cholesterol: 0mg

Sodium: 580mg

Total Carbohydrates: 22g

Dietary Fiber: 5g

Sugars: 11g

Protein: 2g

Ingredients:

- 1 tablespoon olive oil

- 1 onion, diced

- 2 cloves garlic, minced

- 1 tablespoon fresh ginger, grated

- 1 pound carrots, peeled and chopped

- 4 cups vegetable broth

- 1 can (14 ounces) coconut milk

- 1 teaspoon ground turmeric

- 1/2 teaspoon ground cumin

- Salt and pepper to taste

- Optional garnish: fresh cilantro, coconut cream, toasted pumpkin seeds

Tips for Cooking:

- Use fresh ginger for the best flavor in the soup. Peel the ginger using a spoon or vegetable peeler and grate it finely.

- Sauté the diced onion, minced garlic, and grated ginger in olive oil until softened and fragrant before adding the chopped carrots and broth.

- Use vegetable broth for a vegetarian version of the soup, or chicken broth for a non-vegetarian option.

- Simmer the soup until the carrots are tender before blending it until smooth for a creamy texture.

- Stir in coconut milk, ground turmeric, ground cumin, salt, and pepper for added flavor and richness.

- Adjust the seasoning of the soup with additional salt and pepper to taste before serving.

- Garnish the ginger carrot soup with fresh cilantro, a drizzle of coconut cream, or toasted pumpkin seeds for added flavor and texture.

Instructions:

1. Heat olive oil in a large pot over medium heat. Add diced onion to the pot and cook until softened and translucent, about 5 minutes.

2. Add minced garlic and grated ginger to the pot and cook for an additional 1-2 minutes, until fragrant.

3. Stir in chopped carrots and vegetable broth. Bring the mixture to a boil, then reduce the heat to low and simmer, covered, for 20 minutes, or until the carrots are tender.

4. Once the carrots are tender, remove the pot from the heat. Use an immersion blender to blend the soup until smooth and creamy. Alternatively, transfer the soup in batches to a blender and blend until smooth, then return it to the pot.

5. Stir in coconut milk, ground turmeric, ground cumin, salt, and pepper. Return the pot to the stove and simmer the soup over low heat for an additional 5 minutes to allow the flavors to meld.

6. Taste the soup and adjust the seasoning with additional salt and pepper if needed.

7. Ladle the ginger carrot soup into serving bowls. Garnish with fresh cilantro, a drizzle of coconut cream, or toasted pumpkin seeds if desired.

8. Serve the soup hot and enjoy a comforting and flavorful dinner option!

SOFT TOFU STIR-FRY WITH VEGETABLES

Serving: 4 servings   Preparation Time: 15 minutes   Cook Time: 15 minutes

Nutritional Information:

Serving Size: 1 cup

Calories: 180 kcal

Total Fat: 10g

Saturated Fat: 1.5g

Cholesterol: 0mg

Sodium: 450mg

Total Carbohydrates: 15g

Dietary Fiber: 4g

Sugars: 6g

Protein: 12g

Ingredients:

- 1 block (14 ounces) soft tofu, drained and cut into cubes

- 2 tablespoons soy sauce

- 1 tablespoon rice vinegar

- 1 tablespoon sesame oil

- 1 tablespoon olive oil

- 2 cloves garlic, minced

- 1 teaspoon fresh ginger, grated

- 2 cups mixed vegetables (such as bell peppers, broccoli, carrots, snap peas)

- Salt and pepper to taste

- Optional garnish: sliced green onions, toasted sesame seeds

Tips for Cooking:

- Use soft or silken tofu for a creamy texture in the stir-fry.

- Drain the tofu well and pat it dry with paper towels to remove excess moisture before cooking.

- Marinate the tofu cubes in soy sauce, rice vinegar, and sesame oil for at least 15 minutes before cooking to infuse them with flavor.

- Use a non-stick skillet or wok for stir-frying the tofu and vegetables to prevent sticking.

- Stir-fry the tofu over medium-high heat until it is golden brown and crispy on the outside before adding the vegetables.

- Add minced garlic and grated ginger to the skillet for aromatic flavor in the stir-fry.

- Use a variety of colorful vegetables for a visually appealing and nutritious stir-fry.

- Season the stir-fry with soy sauce, salt, and pepper to taste, adjusting the seasoning as needed.

- Garnish the stir-fry with sliced green onions and toasted sesame seeds for added flavor and texture.

Instructions:

1. Drain the block of soft tofu and cut it into cubes. Place the tofu cubes in a shallow dish and add soy sauce, rice vinegar, and sesame oil. Gently toss to coat the tofu evenly in the marinade. Let it marinate for at least 15 minutes.

2. Heat olive oil in a large skillet or wok over medium-high heat. Add minced garlic and grated ginger to the skillet and cook for 1-2 minutes, until fragrant.

3. Add the marinated tofu cubes to the skillet in a single layer. Cook for 5-6 minutes, stirring occasionally, until the tofu is golden brown and crispy on all sides. Remove the tofu from the skillet and set it aside.

4. In the same skillet, add mixed vegetables (such as bell peppers, broccoli, carrots, and snap peas). Stir-fry the vegetables for 4-5 minutes, until they are tender-crisp.

5. Return the cooked tofu to the skillet with the vegetables. Stir to combine and heat through.

6. Season the stir-fry with salt and pepper to taste. Add additional soy sauce if desired.

7. Garnish the soft tofu stir-fry with sliced green onions and toasted sesame seeds.

8. Serve the stir-fry hot over cooked rice or noodles as a delicious and nutritious dinner option!

SOFT POLENTA WITH TOMATO BASIL SAUCE

Serving: 4 servings   Preparation Time: 10 minutes   Cook Time: 30 minutes

Nutritional Information:

Serving Size: 1 cup of polenta with sauce

Calories: 200 kcal

Total Fat: 3g

Saturated Fat: 0.5g

Cholesterol: 0mg

Sodium: 450mg

Total Carbohydrates: 40g

Dietary Fiber: 3g

Sugars: 3g

Protein: 5g

Ingredients:

- 1 cup polenta (cornmeal)

- 4 cups water or vegetable broth

- Salt to taste

- 1 tablespoon olive oil

- 1 onion, finely chopped

- 2 cloves garlic, minced

- 1 can (14 ounces) crushed tomatoes

- 1/4 cup fresh basil leaves, chopped

- Salt and pepper to taste

- Optional garnish: grated Parmesan cheese, additional fresh basil leaves

Tips for Cooking:

- Use coarsely ground polenta (cornmeal) for a creamy and smooth texture.

- Use water or vegetable broth to cook the polenta for added flavor.

- Stir the polenta continuously while cooking to prevent lumps from forming.

- Add salt to the water or broth before adding the polenta for seasoning.

- Cook the polenta over low heat, stirring frequently, until it thickens and becomes creamy.

- In a separate pan, sauté chopped onion and minced garlic in olive oil until softened and fragrant before adding the crushed tomatoes and basil for the sauce.

- Simmer the tomato basil sauce over low heat until it thickens and the flavors meld together, stirring occasionally.

- Season the sauce with salt and pepper to taste before serving over the cooked polenta.

Instructions:

1. In a large saucepan, bring 4 cups of water or vegetable broth to a boil over high heat.

2. Once the liquid is boiling, gradually whisk in 1 cup of polenta (cornmeal) in a steady stream, stirring constantly to prevent lumps from forming.

3. Reduce the heat to low and continue to cook the polenta, stirring frequently, for 20-25 minutes, or until it is thick and creamy.

4. While the polenta is cooking, prepare the tomato basil sauce. Heat olive oil in a separate skillet over medium heat. Add finely chopped onion and minced garlic to the skillet and sauté until softened and fragrant, about 5 minutes.

5. Add the crushed tomatoes and chopped fresh basil leaves to the skillet with the sautéed onion and garlic. Season with salt and pepper to taste. Stir to combine.

6. Simmer the tomato basil sauce over low heat for 10-15 minutes, stirring occasionally, until it thickens slightly and the flavors meld together.

7. Once the polenta is cooked and creamy, remove it from the heat and season with salt to taste.

8. To serve, spoon the cooked polenta into serving bowls and ladle the tomato basil sauce over the top.

9. Garnish with grated Parmesan cheese and additional fresh basil leaves if desired.

10. Serve the soft polenta with tomato basil sauce hot as a delicious and comforting dinner option!

CHAPTER 4

SNACK RECIPES

APPLESAUCE MUFFINS

Serving: 12 muffins   Preparation Time: 10 minutes   Cook Time: 20 minutes

Nutritional Information:

Serving Size: 1 muffin

Calories: 150 kcal

Total Fat: 4g

Saturated Fat: 0.5g

Cholesterol: 15mg

Sodium: 180mg

Total Carbohydrates: 27g

Dietary Fiber: 1g

Sugars: 13g

Protein: 2g

Ingredients:

- 1 1/2 cups all-purpose flour

- 1/2 cup granulated sugar

- 1 teaspoon baking powder

- 1/2 teaspoon baking soda

- 1/4 teaspoon salt

- 1 teaspoon ground cinnamon

- 1/2 teaspoon ground nutmeg

- 1/2 cup unsweetened applesauce

- 1/4 cup vegetable oil

- 1/4 cup milk

- 1 large egg

- 1 teaspoon vanilla extract

- Optional: 1/2 cup chopped nuts or raisins

Tips for Cooking:

- Preheat the oven before mixing the batter to ensure it reaches the correct temperature for baking.

- Use unsweetened applesauce for a healthier option without added sugars.

- Mix the dry ingredients (flour, sugar, baking powder, baking soda, salt, cinnamon, and nutmeg) together in a large bowl before adding the wet ingredients to ensure even distribution of the leavening agents and spices.

- Combine the wet ingredients (applesauce, vegetable oil, milk, egg, and vanilla extract) in a separate bowl before adding them to the dry ingredients.

- Fold in chopped nuts or raisins into the muffin batter for added texture and flavor.

- Fill the muffin cups or liners about two-thirds full with batter to ensure they rise evenly without overflowing.

- Bake the muffins in a preheated oven at 375°F (190°C) for about 18-20 minutes, or until a toothpick inserted into the center comes out clean.

- Allow the muffins to cool in the muffin tin for a few minutes before transferring them to a wire rack to cool completely.

Instructions:

1. Preheat the oven to 375°F (190°C). Line a muffin tin with paper liners or grease with non-stick cooking spray.

2. In a large bowl, whisk together the all-purpose flour, granulated sugar, baking powder, baking soda, salt, ground cinnamon, and ground nutmeg until well combined.

3. In a separate bowl, mix together the unsweetened applesauce, vegetable oil, milk, egg, and vanilla extract until smooth and well combined.

4. Pour the wet ingredients into the dry ingredients and stir until just combined. Do not over mix.

5. If desired, fold in chopped nuts or raisins until evenly distributed throughout the batter.

6. Spoon the batter into the prepared muffin tin, filling each cup about two-thirds full.

7. Bake in the preheated oven for 18-20 minutes, or until a toothpick inserted into the center of a muffin comes out clean.

8. Remove the muffin tin from the oven and allow the muffins to cool in the tin for 5 minutes before transferring them to a wire rack to cool completely.

9. Once cooled, serve the applesauce muffins as a delicious and wholesome snack option!

BAKED APPLE SLICES WITH CINNAMON

Serving: 4 servings   Preparation Time: 10 minutes   Cook Time: 20 minutes

Nutritional Information:

Serving Size: 1/2 cup

Calories: 60 kcal

Total Fat: 0g

Saturated Fat: 0g

Cholesterol: 0mg

Sodium: 0mg

Total Carbohydrates: 16g

Dietary Fiber: 3g

Sugars: 11g

Protein: 0g

Ingredients:

- 4 apples (such as Granny Smith or Honey crisp), cored and sliced

- 1 tablespoon lemon juice

- 1 tablespoon maple syrup or honey (optional)

- 1 teaspoon ground cinnamon

- Optional toppings: chopped nuts, granola, Greek yogurt, or whipped cream

Tips for Cooking:

- Choose firm and crisp apples, such as Granny Smith or Honey crisp, for the best texture when baked.

- Core and slice the apples evenly to ensure they cook uniformly.

- Toss the sliced apples with lemon juice to prevent them from browning and add a touch of acidity.

- For added sweetness, drizzle the sliced apples with maple syrup or honey before baking.

- Sprinkle ground cinnamon over the sliced apples for warm and aromatic flavor.

- Arrange the sliced apples in a single layer on a baking sheet lined with parchment paper or aluminum foil to prevent sticking.

- Bake the apple slices in a preheated oven at 375°F (190°C) until they are tender and caramelized, stirring halfway through cooking for even browning.

- Serve the baked apple slices warm with your favorite toppings, such as chopped nuts, granola, Greek yogurt, or whipped cream, for added flavor and texture.

Instructions:

1. Preheat the oven to 375°F (190°C). Line a baking sheet with parchment paper or aluminum foil for easy cleanup.

2. Core and slice the apples into even thickness, about 1/4 inches thick.

3. In a large bowl, toss the sliced apples with lemon juice to coat evenly and prevent browning.

4. If desired, drizzle the sliced apples with maple syrup or honey, and sprinkle with ground cinnamon. Toss to coat evenly.

5. Arrange the coated apple slices in a single layer on the prepared baking sheet.

6. Bake in the preheated oven for 18-20 minutes, or until the apple slices are tender and caramelized, stirring halfway through cooking for even browning.

7. Once baked, remove the apple slices from the oven and let them cool slightly.

8. Serve the baked apple slices warm as a delicious and healthy snack option!

9. Optionally, top the baked apple slices with your favorite toppings, such as chopped nuts, granola, Greek yogurt, or whipped cream, for added flavor and texture.

EGG DROP SOUP

Serving: 4 servings   Preparation Time: 5 minutes   Cook Time: 10 minutes

Nutritional Information:

Serving Size: 1 cup

Calories: 70 kcal

Total Fat: 3g

Saturated Fat: 1g

Cholesterol: 100mg

Sodium: 780mg

Total Carbohydrates: 3g

Dietary Fiber: 0g

Sugars: 1g

Protein: 7g

Ingredients:

- 4 cups chicken broth

- 2 eggs

- 2 green onions, thinly sliced

- 1 tablespoon soy sauce

- 1/2 teaspoon ground ginger

- Salt and pepper to taste

- Optional garnish: chopped fresh cilantro or sliced green onions

Tips for Cooking:

- Use high-quality chicken broth or homemade broth for the best flavor in the egg drop soup.

- Beat the eggs well in a separate bowl before adding them to the hot broth to ensure even distribution when they are dropped into the soup.

- Use thinly sliced green onions for a mild onion flavor and added texture in the soup.

- Season the soup with soy sauce, ground ginger, salt, and pepper for a savory and aromatic broth.

- Bring the chicken broth to a gentle simmer before adding the beaten eggs in a slow, steady stream to create delicate ribbons.

- Stir the soup gently in one direction while adding the beaten eggs to encourage them to form wispy ribbons.

- Avoid stirring the soup vigorously once the eggs are added to prevent them from breaking up into small pieces.

- Adjust the seasoning of the soup with additional soy sauce, salt, and pepper to taste before serving.

- Garnish the egg drop soup with chopped fresh cilantro or sliced green onions for added freshness and color.

Instructions:

1. In a large pot, bring 4 cups of chicken broth to a gentle simmer over medium heat.

2. While the broth is heating, beat the eggs in a small bowl until well combined.

3. Once the broth is simmering, add thinly sliced green onions, soy sauce, and ground ginger to the pot. Stir to combine.

4. Slowly pour the beaten eggs into the simmering broth in a thin, steady stream while stirring the soup gently in one direction.

5. Continue stirring the soup gently for about 1 minute, until the eggs form wispy ribbons.

6. Season the egg drop soup with salt and pepper to taste. Adjust the seasoning with additional soy sauce, if desired.

7. Once the soup is seasoned to your liking, remove the pot from the heat.

8. Ladle the egg drop soup into serving bowls and garnish with chopped fresh cilantro or sliced green onions, if desired.

9. Serve the egg drop soup hot as a comforting and flavorful snack option!

SOFT BAKED APPLES WITH GREEK YOGURT

Serving: 4 servings   Preparation Time: 10 minutes   Cook Time: 25 minutes

Nutritional Information:

Serving Size: 1 apple

Calories: 120 kcal

Total Fat: 2g

Saturated Fat: 1g

Cholesterol: 5mg

Sodium: 20mg

Total Carbohydrates: 25g

Dietary Fiber: 4g

Sugars: 18g

Protein: 3g

Ingredients:

- 4 apples (such as Honey crisp or Gala), cored

- 1 tablespoon unsalted butter, melted

- 1 tablespoon honey or maple syrup

- 1 teaspoon ground cinnamon

- 1/4 teaspoon ground nutmeg

- 1/4 cup chopped nuts (such as walnuts or pecans)

- 1 cup Greek yogurt

Tips for Cooking:

- Choose firm and slightly tart apples such as Honey crisp or Gala, for the best texture and flavor when baked.

- Core the apples evenly to create a well for the filling without cutting all the way through.

- Brush the inside of the cored apples with melted butter to help them brown and become tender when baked.

- Drizzle honey or maple syrup over the apples for added sweetness and flavor before sprinkling with cinnamon and nutmeg.

- Top the stuffed apples with chopped nuts for added texture and crunch.

- Bake the stuffed apples in a preheated oven until they are tender and caramelized, checking for doneness with a fork.

- Serve the soft baked apples warm with a dollop of Greek yogurt for a creamy and tangy contrast.

Instructions:

1. Preheat the oven to 375°F (190°C). Line a baking dish with parchment paper or aluminum foil for easy cleanup.

2. Core the apples using an apple corer or a small knife, making sure to remove the seeds and create a well in the center without cutting all the way through the bottom.

3. In a small bowl, mix together the melted butter and honey or maple syrup until well combined.

4. Brush the inside of each cored apple with the butter and honey mixture, coating evenly.

5. In another small bowl, combine the ground cinnamon and ground nutmeg.

6. Sprinkle the cinnamon and nutmeg mixture evenly over the buttered and honeyed apples.

7. Place the stuffed apples in the prepared baking dish. Fill each apple with chopped nuts, dividing evenly among them.

8. Bake the stuffed apples in the preheated oven for 20-25 minutes, or until the apples are tender and caramelized, and the nuts are toasted.

9. Once baked, remove the stuffed apples from the oven and let them cool slightly.

10. Serve the soft baked apples warm with a dollop of Greek yogurt on top for a creamy and tangy contrast.

11. Enjoy these delicious soft baked apples with Greek yogurt as a wholesome and satisfying snack!

OATMEAL BANANA COOKIES

Serving: 12 cookies   Preparation Time: 10 minutes   Cook Time: 12 minutes

Nutritional Information:

Serving Size: 1 cookie

Calories: 90 kcal

Total Fat: 2g

Saturated Fat: 0.5g

Cholesterol: 5mg

Sodium: 30mg

Total Carbohydrates: 17g

Dietary Fiber: 1g

Sugars: 7g

Protein: 2g

Ingredients:

- 2 ripe bananas, mashed

- 1 cup old-fashioned oats

- 1/4 cup almond flour or whole wheat flour

- 1/4 cup unsweetened shredded coconut

- 1/4 cup raisins or chocolate chips (optional)

- 1 teaspoon ground cinnamon

- 1/2 teaspoon vanilla extract

- Pinch of salt

Tips for Cooking:

- Use ripe bananas with brown spots for the best flavor and sweetness in the cookies.

- Mash the bananas well with a fork or potato masher until smooth and no large lumps remain.

- Use old-fashioned oats for a chewy texture in the cookies.

- Add almond flour or whole-wheat flour to bind the ingredients together and add a nutty flavor.

- Include unsweetened shredded coconut for added texture and a hint of sweetness in the cookies.

- For extra sweetness, add raisins or chocolate chips to the cookie dough before baking.

- Season the cookie dough with ground cinnamon, vanilla extract, and a pinch of salt for flavor enhancement.

- Use a cookie scoop or tablespoon to portion the cookie dough onto a baking sheet lined with parchment paper for even-sized cookies.

- Flatten the cookie dough slightly with the back of a spoon or your fingers before baking to ensure even cooking.

- Bake the oatmeal banana cookies in a preheated oven until they are golden brown and firm to the touch.

- Let the cookies cool on the baking sheet for a few minutes before transferring them to a wire rack to cool completely.

Instructions:

1. Preheat the oven to 350°F (175°C). Line a baking sheet with parchment paper or lightly grease it with cooking spray.

2. In a large mixing bowl, combine mashed bananas, old-fashioned oats, almond flour or whole wheat flour, unsweetened shredded coconut, raisins or chocolate chips (if using), ground cinnamon, vanilla extract, and a pinch of salt. Mix until well combined.

3. Using a cookie scoop or tablespoon, drop spoonful of the cookie dough onto the prepared baking sheet, spacing them apart to allow for spreading during baking.

4. Use the back of a spoon or your fingers to flatten each cookie slightly.

5. Bake in the preheated oven for 10-12 minutes, or until the cookies are golden brown and firm to the touch.

6. Remove the baking sheet from the oven and let the cookies cool on it for 5 minutes.

7. Transfer the cookies to a wire rack to cool completely before serving.

8. Enjoy these delicious oatmeal banana cookies as a wholesome and satisfying snack!

PUMPKIN SPICE SMOOTHIE

Serving: 2 servings   Preparation Time: 5 minutes

Nutritional Information:

Serving Size: 1 smoothie

Calories: 180 kcal

Total Fat: 5g

Saturated Fat: 1g

Cholesterol: 0mg

Sodium: 150mg

Total Carbohydrates: 30g

Dietary Fiber: 6g

Sugars: 18g

Protein: 5g

Ingredients:

- 1 cup unsweetened almond milk (or any milk of choice)

- 1 ripe banana, frozen

- 1/2 cup canned pumpkin puree

- 1/4 cup plain Greek yogurt

- 2 tablespoons maple syrup or honey

- 1/2 teaspoon ground cinnamon

- 1/4 teaspoon ground nutmeg

- 1/4 teaspoon ground ginger

- 1/4 teaspoon vanilla extract

- Ice cubes (optional)

Tips for Cooking:

- Use unsweetened almond milk or any milk of your choice for a creamy base in the smoothie.

- Freeze ripe bananas beforehand for a thicker and creamier texture in the smoothie.

- Canned pumpkin puree adds a velvety texture and delicious flavor to the smoothie.

- Plain Greek yogurt adds creaminess and a protein boost to the smoothie.

- Sweeten the smoothie with maple syrup or honey to taste, adjusting the amount based on personal preference.

- Blend in ground cinnamon, ground nutmeg, ground ginger, and vanilla extract for warm and aromatic pumpkin spice flavor.

- For a thicker consistency, add ice cubes to the smoothie before blending.

- Garnish the smoothie with a sprinkle of ground cinnamon or a dollop of whipped cream for an extra treat.

Instructions:

1. In a blender, combine unsweetened almond milk, frozen banana, canned pumpkin puree, plain Greek yogurt, maple syrup or honey, ground cinnamon, ground nutmeg, ground ginger, and vanilla extract.

2. If desired, add ice cubes to the blender for a thicker consistency.

3. Blend all the ingredients on high speed until smooth and creamy.

4. Stop and scrape down the sides of the blender as needed to ensure all ingredients are well incorporated.

5. Once the smoothie reaches your desired consistency, taste and adjust the sweetness or spice level if necessary.

6. Pour the pumpkin spice smoothie into glasses.

7. Optionally, garnish with a sprinkle of ground cinnamon or a dollop of whipped cream.

8. Serve the smoothie immediately and enjoy the delightful flavors of pumpkin spice in a refreshing and nutritious snack!

DESSERT RECIPES

POACHED PEAR WITH HONEY AND CINNAMON

Serving: 4 servings   Preparation Time: 10 minutes   Cook Time: 30 minutes

Nutritional Information:

Serving Size: 1 poached pear

Calories: 120 kcal

Total Fat: 0g

Saturated Fat: 0g

Cholesterol: 0mg

Sodium: 5mg

Total Carbohydrates: 31g

Dietary Fiber: 5g

Sugars: 23g

Protein: 1g

Ingredients:

- 4 ripe pears, peeled, halved, and cored

- 4 cups water

- 1/2 cup honey

- 2 cinnamon sticks

- 1 teaspoon vanilla extract

- Optional garnish: chopped nuts, whipped cream, or Greek yogurt

Tips for Cooking:

- Choose ripe but firm pears for poaching to ensure they hold their shape during cooking.

- Peel the pears, leaving the stem intact if desired for an elegant presentation.

- Core the pears carefully to remove the seeds and tough center without breaking the fruit.

- Use a large saucepan or pot to poach the pears, ensuring they are fully submerged in the poaching liquid.

- Poach the pears in a mixture of water, honey, cinnamon sticks, and vanilla extract for a sweet and aromatic flavor.

- Bring the poaching liquid to a gentle simmer before adding the pears to prevent them from cooking unevenly.

- Simmer the pears over low heat, covered, until they are tender and infused with the flavors of honey and cinnamon.

- Rotate the pears occasionally during cooking to ensure they cook evenly on all sides.

- Once poached, let the pears cool in the poaching liquid to absorb more flavor before serving.

- Serve the poached pears warm or chilled, garnished with chopped nuts, whipped cream, or Greek yogurt for added texture and richness.

Instructions:

1. In a large saucepan or pot, combine water, honey, cinnamon sticks, and vanilla extract. Stir to combine.

2. Place the saucepan over medium heat and bring the poaching liquid to a gentle simmer, stirring occasionally until the honey is dissolved.

3. While the poaching liquid is heating, prepare the pears. Peel the pears and cut them in half lengthwise. Use a melon baller or spoon to remove the core and seeds from each half, creating a cavity for the poaching liquid.

4. Once the poaching liquid is simmering, carefully add the prepared pear halves to the saucepan, ensuring they are fully submerged in the liquid.

5. Reduce the heat to low, cover the saucepan, and simmer the pears gently for 20-25 minutes, or until they are tender when pierced with a fork.

6. Rotate the pears occasionally during cooking to ensure they cook evenly and absorb the flavors of the poaching liquid.

7. Once the pears are tender, remove the saucepan from the heat and let the pears cool in the poaching liquid for 10-15 minutes to absorb more flavor.

8. Using a slotted spoon, carefully transfer the poached pears to serving plates or bowls, arranging them cut-side up.

9. Optionally, drizzle some of the poaching liquid over the pears for added sweetness and flavor.

10. Garnish the poached pears with chopped nuts, a dollop of whipped cream, or a spoonful of Greek yogurt, if desired.

11. Serve the poached pears warm or chilled as a delightful and elegant dessert option!

COCONUT MILK RICE PUDDING

Serving: 6 servings   Preparation Time: 5 minutes   Cook Time: 30 minutes

Nutritional Information:

Serving Size: 1/2 cup

Calories: 150 kcal

Total Fat: 5g

Saturated Fat: 4g

Cholesterol: 0mg

Sodium: 10mg

Total Carbohydrates: 25g

Dietary Fiber: 1g

Sugars: 15g

Protein: 2g

Ingredients:

- 1 cup white rice (such as jasmine or basmati)

- 2 cups water

- 1 can (13.5 oz) coconut milk

- 1/4 cup granulated sugar

- 1 teaspoon vanilla extract

- Pinch of salt

- Optional toppings: toasted coconut flakes, sliced almonds, or fresh fruit

Tips for Cooking:

- Rinse the rice under cold water before cooking to remove excess starch and prevent the pudding from becoming too sticky.

- Use jasmine or basmati rice for a fragrant and fluffy texture in the pudding.

- Combine water and coconut milk for a creamy and coconut-flavored base in the pudding.

- Add granulated sugar for sweetness, adjusting the amount based on personal preference.

- Enhance the flavor of the pudding with vanilla extract and a pinch of salt.

- Stir the pudding occasionally while cooking to prevent it from sticking to the bottom of the pot.

- Cook the pudding over low heat, stirring frequently, to allow the rice to absorb the coconut milk mixture slowly.

- Remove the pudding from the heat when the rice is tender and the mixture has thickened to your desired consistency.

- Let the pudding cool slightly before serving to allow it to thicken further.

- Serve the coconut milk rice pudding warm or chilled, topped with toasted coconut flakes, sliced almonds, or fresh fruit for added flavor and texture.

Instructions:

1. In a medium saucepan, combine the white rice and water. Bring to a boil over medium-high heat.

2. Reduce the heat to low, cover the saucepan, and simmer the rice for 15 minutes, or until most of the water is absorbed and the rice is tender.

3. Stir in the coconut milk, granulated sugar, vanilla extract, and a pinch of salt. Mix well to combine.

4. Continue to cook the pudding over low heat, stirring frequently, for another 10-15 minutes, or until the mixture thickens and the rice is fully cooked.

5. Remove the saucepan from the heat and let the pudding cool slightly.

6. Serve the coconut milk rice pudding warm or chilled, topped with toasted coconut flakes, sliced almonds, or fresh fruit, if desired.

7. Enjoy this creamy and comforting coconut milk rice pudding as a delightful dessert option!

SOFT BAKED PEAR WITH ALMOND CRUMBLE

Serving: 4 servings   Preparation Time: 10 minutes   Cook Time: 25 minutes

Nutritional Information:

Serving Size: 1 pear with almond crumble

Calories: 200 kcal

Total Fat: 9g

Saturated Fat: 2g

Cholesterol: 0mg

Sodium: 5mg

Total Carbohydrates: 29g

Dietary Fiber: 5g

Sugars: 17g

Protein: 3g

Ingredients:

- 4 ripe pears, halved and cored

- 1/2 cup almond flour or almond meal

- 1/4 cup rolled oats

- 1/4 cup chopped almonds

- 2 tablespoons honey or maple syrup

- 2 tablespoons coconut oil, melted

- 1/2 teaspoon ground cinnamon

- Pinch of salt

- Optional garnish: vanilla ice cream or whipped cream

Tips for Cooking:

- Choose ripe but firm pears for baking to ensure they hold their shape and texture.

- Halve and core the pears carefully to create a well for the almond crumble without breaking the fruit.

- Combine almond flour or almond meal, rolled oats, chopped almonds, honey or maple syrup, melted coconut oil, ground cinnamon, and a pinch of salt for the almond crumble topping.

- Mix the almond crumble topping until it resembles coarse crumbs, ensuring all ingredients are evenly incorporated.

- Fill the cavities of the halved pears with the almond crumble mixture, pressing gently to adhere.

- Bake the stuffed pears in a preheated oven until they are tender and the almond crumble is golden brown and crisp.

- Serve the soft baked pears warm with a scoop of vanilla ice cream or a dollop of whipped cream for a delightful dessert.

Instructions:

1. Preheat the oven to 375°F (190°C). Line a baking dish with parchment paper or lightly grease it with cooking spray.

2. Halve the ripe pears lengthwise and use a spoon or melon baller to carefully remove the cores and seeds, creating a well in each pear half.

3. In a mixing bowl, combine almond flour or almond meal, rolled oats, chopped almonds, honey or maple syrup, melted coconut oil, ground cinnamon, and a pinch of salt. Mix well until the ingredients are evenly incorporated and the mixture resembles coarse crumbs.

4. Place the pear halves, cut side up, in the prepared baking dish. Fill the cavities of each pear half with the almond crumble mixture, pressing gently to adhere.

5. Bake the stuffed pears in the preheated oven for 20-25 minutes, or until the pears are tender and the almond crumble topping is golden brown and crisp.

6. Remove the baking dish from the oven and let the stuffed pears cool slightly.

7. Serve the soft baked pears warm, garnished with a scoop of vanilla ice cream or a dollop of whipped cream, if desired.

8. Enjoy the delightful combination of tender baked pears and crunchy almond crumble for a delicious dessert!

BONUS RECIPES

CREAMY CAULIFLOWER MASH

Serving: 4 servings   Preparation Time: 10 minutes   Cook Time: 20 minutes

Nutritional Information:

Serving Size: 1/2 cup

Calories: 60 kcal

Total Fat: 3g

Saturated Fat: 2g

Cholesterol: 10mg

Sodium: 150mg

Total Carbohydrates: 7g

Dietary Fiber: 3g

Sugars: 3g

Protein: 3g

Ingredients:

- 1 medium head cauliflower, cut into florets

- 2 cloves garlic, minced

- 2 tablespoons unsalted butter

- 1/4 cup grated Parmesan cheese

- 1/4 cup heavy cream

- Salt and pepper to taste

- Optional garnish: chopped fresh parsley or chives

Tips for Cooking:

- Use fresh cauliflower for the best flavor and texture in the mash.

- Cut the cauliflower into evenly sized florets for even cooking.

- Steam the cauliflower instead of boiling to retain more nutrients and prevent the mash from becoming too watery.

- Cook the cauliflower until it is very tender and easily pierced with a fork for a smooth and creamy texture.

- Drain the cooked cauliflower well to remove excess moisture before mashing.

- Use a food processor or immersion blender to puree the cauliflower until smooth and creamy.

- Add minced garlic, unsalted butter, grated Parmesan cheese, and heavy cream for rich and flavorful cauliflower mash.

- Season the mash with salt and pepper to taste, adjusting the amount based on personal preference.

- Garnish the creamy cauliflower mash with chopped fresh parsley or chives for added color and freshness.

Instructions:

1. Place the cauliflower florets in a steamer basket over a pot of boiling water. Cover and steam for 10-12 minutes, or until the cauliflower is very tender when pierced with a fork.

2. Drain the steamed cauliflower well and transfer it to a food processor or large mixing bowl.

3. Add minced garlic, unsalted butter, grated Parmesan cheese, and heavy cream to the steamed cauliflower.

4. Process or blend the cauliflower mixture until smooth and creamy, scraping down the sides of the food processor or bowl as needed.

5. Season the creamy cauliflower mash with salt and pepper to taste, adjusting the seasoning as needed.

6. Transfer the creamy cauliflower mash to a serving dish and garnish with chopped fresh parsley or chives, if desired.

7. Serve the creamy cauliflower mash warm as a delicious and nutritious side dish or bonus recipe option!

SPINACH AND FETA OMELETTE

Serving: 1 serving   Preparation Time: 5 minutes   Cook Time: 5 minutes

Nutritional Information:

Serving Size: 1 omelette

Calories: 250 kcal

Total Fat: 18g

Saturated Fat: 8g

Cholesterol: 380mg

Sodium: 550mg

Total Carbohydrates: 4g

Dietary Fiber: 1g

Sugars: 2g

Protein: 17g

Ingredients:

- 2 large eggs

- 1/4 cup chopped fresh spinach

- 2 tablespoons crumbled feta cheese

- 1 tablespoon olive oil or butter

- Salt and pepper to taste

- Optional toppings: chopped tomatoes, sliced avocado, or fresh herbs

Tips for Cooking:

- Use fresh and high-quality eggs for the best flavor and texture in the omelette.

- Beat the eggs well in a bowl until smooth and frothy for a fluffy omelette.

- Chop the fresh spinach finely for even distribution throughout the omelette.

- Crumble the feta cheese into small pieces for easy melting and flavor dispersal.

- Heat the olive oil or butter in a non-stick skillet over medium heat for a golden and crispy omelette.

- Pour the beaten eggs into the hot skillet and cook until the edges start to set before adding the spinach and feta cheese.

- Season the omelette with salt and pepper to taste, adjusting the seasoning based on personal preference.

- Fold the omelette in half using a spatula for a classic presentation, or roll it up for a different presentation.

- Top the cooked omelette with chopped tomatoes, sliced avocado, or fresh herbs for added flavor and freshness.

Instructions:

1. In a bowl, beat the eggs until smooth and frothy. Season with salt and pepper to taste.

2. Heat the olive oil or butter in a non-stick skillet over medium heat.

3. Pour the beaten eggs into the skillet and cook for 1-2 minutes, or until the edges start to set.

4. Sprinkle chopped fresh spinach and crumbled feta cheese evenly over one-half of the omelette.

5. Cook for an additional 1-2 minutes, or until the eggs are set and the cheese starts to melt.

6. Using a spatula, carefully fold the empty half of the omelette over the filling to create a half-moon shape.

7. Cook for another 1-2 minutes, or until the omelette is cooked through and golden brown on both sides.

8. Slide the cooked omelette onto a plate and garnish with chopped tomatoes, sliced avocado, or fresh herbs, if desired.

9. Serve the spinach and feta omelette warm as a delicious and satisfying bonus recipe option!

STEAMED SPINACH AND GARLIC

Serving: 4 servings   Preparation Time: 5 minutes   Cook Time: 5 minutes

Nutritional Information:

Serving Size: 1/2 cup

Calories: 30 kcal

Total Fat: 0g

Saturated Fat: 0g

Cholesterol: 0mg

Sodium: 50mg

Total Carbohydrates: 6g

Dietary Fiber: 3g

Sugars: 1g

Protein: 3g

Ingredients:

- 1 bunch fresh spinach, washed and trimmed

- 2 cloves garlic, minced

- 1 tablespoon olive oil

- Salt and pepper to taste

- Optional garnish: lemon zest or grated Parmesan cheese

Tips for Cooking:

- Use fresh and tender spinach leaves for the best texture and flavor in the dish.

- Wash the spinach thoroughly to remove any dirt or grit, and trim off any tough stems.

- Steam the spinach briefly to preserve its vibrant green color and crisp texture.

- Mince the garlic finely for even distribution throughout the dish.

- Heat the olive oil in a skillet over medium heat before adding the minced garlic to prevent it from burning.

- Season the steamed spinach with salt and pepper to taste, adjusting the seasoning based on personal preference.

- Garnish the dish with lemon zest or grated Parmesan cheese for added flavor and freshness.

Instructions:

1. Wash the fresh spinach thoroughly under cold water to remove any dirt or grit. Trim off any tough stems.

2. Bring a pot of water to a boil over high heat. Place a steamer basket or colander over the pot.

3. Once the water is boiling, add the spinach to the steamer basket or colander. Cover and steam for 2-3 minutes, or until the spinach is wilted and tender.

4. While the spinach is steaming, heat the olive oil in a skillet over medium heat. Add the minced garlic and sauté for 1-2 minutes, or until fragrant and golden brown.

5. Transfer the steamed spinach to a serving dish and drizzle the garlic-infused olive oil over the top.

6. Season the steamed spinach with salt and pepper to taste, tossing gently to coat evenly.

7. Garnish the dish with lemon zest or grated Parmesan cheese, if desired, for added flavor and freshness.

8. Serve the steamed spinach with garlic warm as a delicious and nutritious bonus recipe option!

CHAPTER 7

A 28-DAY MEAL PLAN

Day 1:

Breakfast: Soft Scrambled Eggs, Banana Oatmeal Smoothie

Lunch: Vegetable Soup with Rice

Dinner: Baked Chicken Breast with Herbs, Steamed Spinach with Garlic

Day 2:

Breakfast: Blueberry Banana Smoothie Bowl

Lunch: Turkey Chili with Sweet Potatoes

Dinner: Quinoa Pilaf with Roasted Vegetables

Day 3:

Breakfast: Cottage Cheese Pancakes

Lunch: Lentil Soup with Spinach

Dinner: Soft Polenta with Tomato Basil Sauce

Day 4:

Breakfast: Soft Quinoa Porridge

Lunch: Rice Congee with Chicken

Dinner: Ginger Carrot Soup, Baked Sweet Potato Fries

Day 5:

Breakfast: Avocado and Chicken Salad

Lunch: Turkey Meatballs in Tomato Sauce

Dinner: Spinach and Feta Omelette, Steamed Spinach with Garlic

Day 6:

Breakfast: Creamy Mashed Potatoes

Lunch: Vegetable Soup with Rice

Dinner: Baked Chicken Breast with Herbs, Quinoa Pilaf with Roasted Vegetables

Day 7:

Breakfast: Banana Oatmeal Smoothie

Lunch: Lentil Soup with Spinach

Dinner: Soft Polenta with Tomato Basil Sauce, Steamed Spinach with Garlic

Day 8:

Breakfast: Blueberry Banana Smoothie Bowl

Lunch: Turkey Chili with Sweet Potatoes

Dinner: Ginger Carrot Soup, Baked Sweet Potato Fries

Day 9:

Breakfast: Cottage Cheese Pancakes

Lunch: Rice Congee with Chicken

Dinner: Spinach and Feta Omelette, Steamed Spinach with Garlic

Day 10:

Breakfast: Soft Quinoa Porridge

Lunch: Vegetable Soup with Rice

Dinner: Baked Chicken Breast with Herbs, Quinoa Pilaf with Roasted Vegetables

Day 11:

Breakfast: Avocado and Chicken Salad

Lunch: Lentil Soup with Spinach

Dinner: Soft Polenta with Tomato Basil Sauce, Steamed Spinach with Garlic

Day 12:

Breakfast: Creamy Mashed Potatoes

Lunch: Turkey Meatballs in Tomato Sauce

Dinner: Ginger Carrot Soup, Baked Sweet Potato Fries

Day 13:

Breakfast: Banana Oatmeal Smoothie

Lunch: Rice Congee with Chicken

Dinner: Spinach and Feta Omelette, Steamed Spinach with Garlic

Day 14:

Breakfast: Blueberry Banana Smoothie Bowl

Lunch: Vegetable Soup with Rice

Dinner: Baked Chicken Breast with Herbs, Quinoa Pilaf with Roasted Vegetables

Day 15:

Breakfast: Soft Scrambled Eggs

Lunch: Lentil Soup with Spinach

Dinner: Soft Polenta with Tomato Basil Sauce, Steamed Spinach with Garlic

Day 16:

Breakfast: Cottage Cheese Pancakes

Lunch: Turkey Chili with Sweet Potatoes

Dinner: Ginger Carrot Soup, Baked Sweet Potato Fries

Day 17:

Breakfast: Soft Quinoa Porridge

Lunch: Rice Congee with Chicken

Dinner: Spinach and Feta Omelette, Steamed Spinach with Garlic

Day 18:

Breakfast: Creamy Mashed Potatoes

Lunch: Vegetable Soup with Rice

Dinner: Baked Chicken Breast with Herbs, Quinoa Pilaf with Roasted Vegetables

Day 19:

Breakfast: Avocado and Chicken Salad

Lunch: Lentil Soup with Spinach

Dinner: Soft Polenta with Tomato Basil Sauce, Steamed Spinach with Garlic

Day 20:

Breakfast: Banana Oatmeal Smoothie

Lunch: Turkey Meatballs in Tomato Sauce

Dinner: Ginger Carrot Soup, Baked Sweet Potato Fries

Day 21:

Breakfast: Blueberry Banana Smoothie Bowl

Lunch: Rice Congee with Chicken

Dinner: Spinach and Feta Omelette, Steamed Spinach with Garlic

Day 22:

Breakfast: Soft Quinoa Porridge

Lunch: Vegetable Soup with Rice

Dinner: Baked Chicken Breast with Herbs, Quinoa Pilaf with Roasted Vegetables

Day 23:

Breakfast: Avocado and Chicken Salad

Lunch: Lentil Soup with Spinach

Dinner: Soft Polenta with Tomato Basil Sauce, Steamed Spinach with Garlic

Day 24:

Breakfast: Creamy Mashed Potatoes

Lunch: Turkey Chili with Sweet Potatoes

Dinner: Ginger Carrot Soup, Baked Sweet Potato Fries

Day 25:

Breakfast: Banana Oatmeal Smoothie

Lunch: Rice Congee with Chicken

Dinner: Spinach and Feta Omelette, Steamed Spinach with Garlic

Day 26:

Breakfast: Blueberry Banana Smoothie Bowl

Lunch: Vegetable Soup with Rice

Dinner: Baked Chicken Breast with Herbs, Quinoa Pilaf with Roasted Vegetables

Day 27:

Breakfast: Soft Scrambled Eggs

Lunch: Lentil Soup with Spinach

Dinner: Soft Polenta with Tomato Basil Sauce, Steamed Spinach with Garlic

Day 28:

Breakfast: Cottage Cheese Pancakes

Lunch: Turkey Meatballs in Tomato Sauce

Dinner: Spinach and Feta Omelette, Steamed Spinach with Garlic

Printed in Great Britain
by Amazon

38405754R00051